LAFF WITH OLAF

& others

A mixed bag of cartoons

RAYMOND BUCKLAND

QVP

Queen Victoria Press

LAFF WITH OLAF & OTHERS
Copyright © Raymond Buckland 2017

ISBN 978-0-9978481-6-8

Queen Victoria Press
153 East South Street, Ste. 892
Wooster, OII 44691-0892

Dedicated to my father and to my wife, Tara

Introduction

Many of these cartoons were drawn back in the 1950s, when I was working in London as an engineering draughtsman with the firm of Rendel, Palmer & Tritton. Later ones were done when I was at British Airways, in New York, in the 1960s and early 1970s.

Some of them were "finished" – ready for publication in various newspapers and magazines – while others were, and are, (obviously, I think) drawn on odd pieces of paper as the ideas struck me. The latter I have left rough, rather than "clean up", since they seem to reflect the casualness in which they were created, though I regret the poor reproduction of some of these. Most of the Olaf ones are of this rough ilk. I had thought to do a series of Olaf cartoons and submit them to some journal, but never actually got around to the submission part of things. Of the various airplane cartoons ("airtoons"?): some of these were published in newsletters of one of the Experimental Aircraft Association chapters in the 1990s.

The originals of some of the cartoons were done in color. I very much wish I could have had them printed in color here, but CreateSpace (the publishing arm I use) does not have any way of printing a book with some of its pages in color and others in black-and-white. Too bad! Some of the colors were very vivid and added a great deal to the artwork, in my opinion.

I first started drawing cartoons when I was about six or seven years old. I used to do all of the Disney characters and then began to create my own. Years later I became more serious with my art, illustrating filmstrips and books (including all of my own books). I took some classes at the London School of Art, and I actually helped pay for my family to emigrate from England and journey to the

United States by doing nearly four hundred detailed illustrations for a science encyclopedia, back in 1961.

I had wanted to get into cartoon movies but had no luck, there being few openings for that in England in those days. I did briefly have my own business as a commercial artist, doing letterheads, advertisements, and the like. I did a lot for Howard Johnson restaurant advertising in the early 1970s.

Humor has always been a big part of my life, and always will be. I hope you get a chuckle from these bits and pieces from my past.

Raymond Buckland

HELP

BUCKAND

"DON'T LEAN OVER TOO FAR...."

"QUICK, GLADYS, — THE WEED-KILLER!"

"EXHIBIT 732 .... MEXICAN RAIN GOD"

"SO MUCH FOR THE SO-CALLED 'CURSE'!"

"HOLD ON TIGHT DEAR, HERE COMES ANOTHER SHARP CORNER!"

"QUITE FRANKLY WE'RE NOT GREATLY INTERESTED IN AUTOBIOGRAPHIES----!"

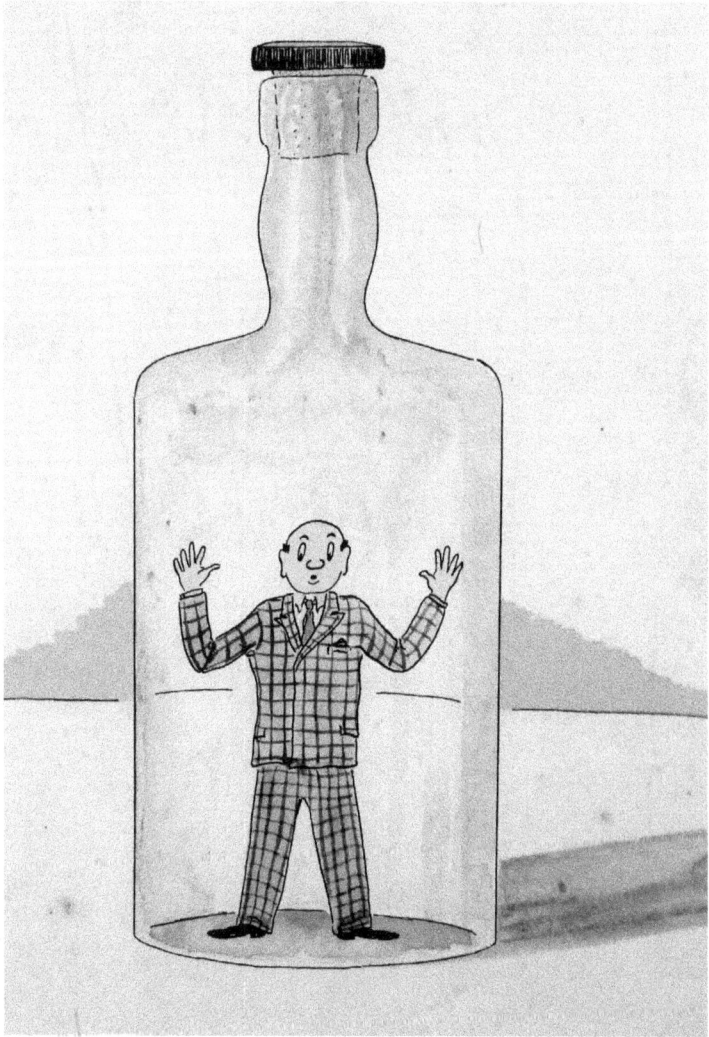

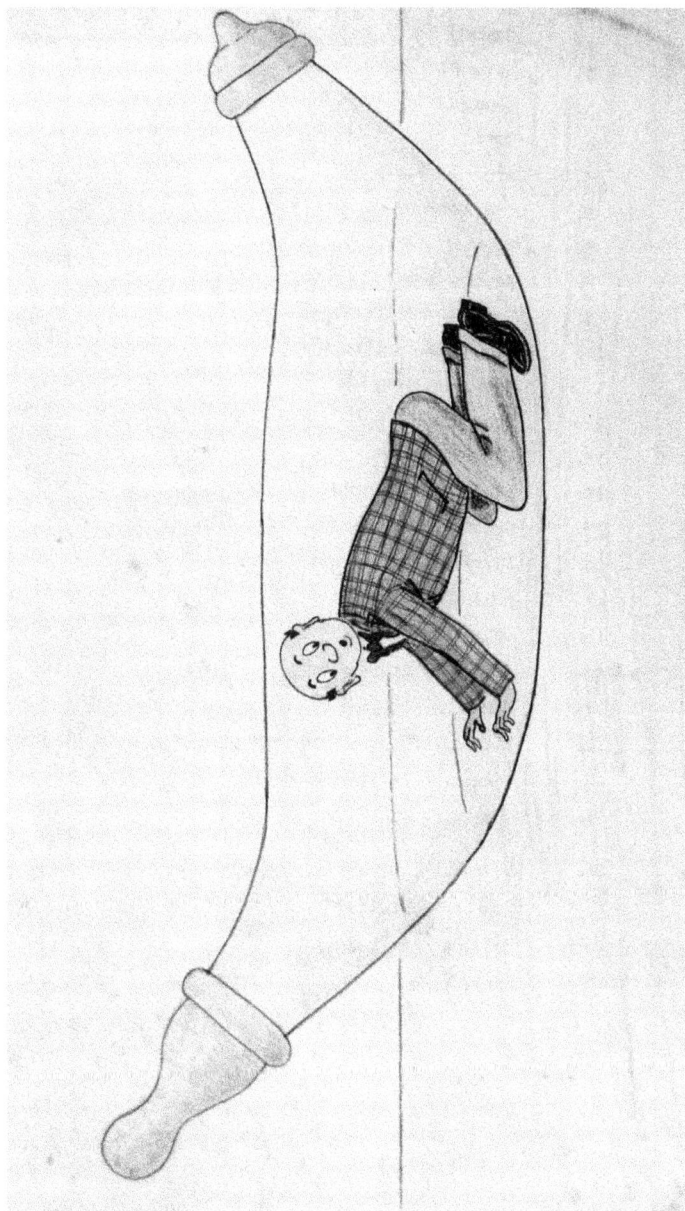

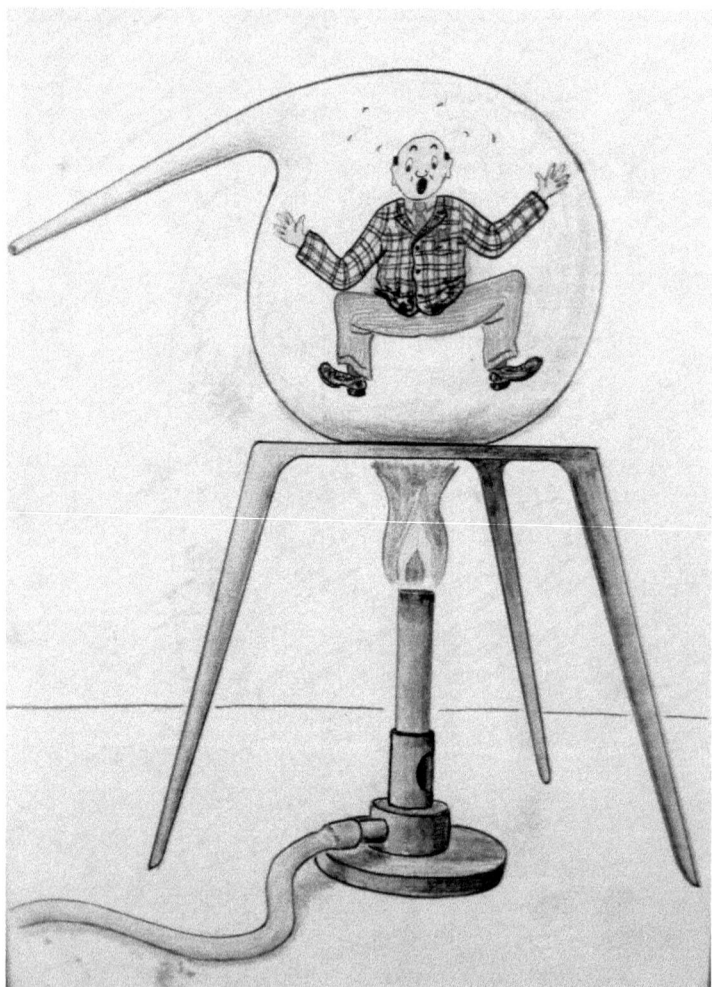

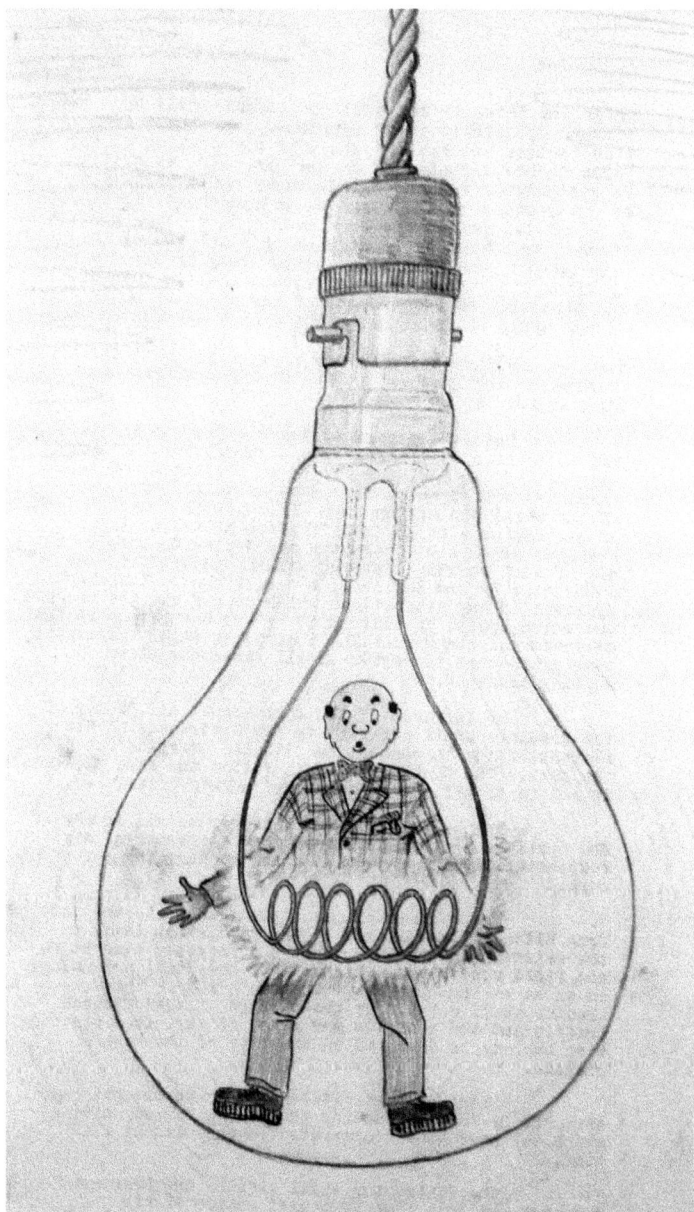

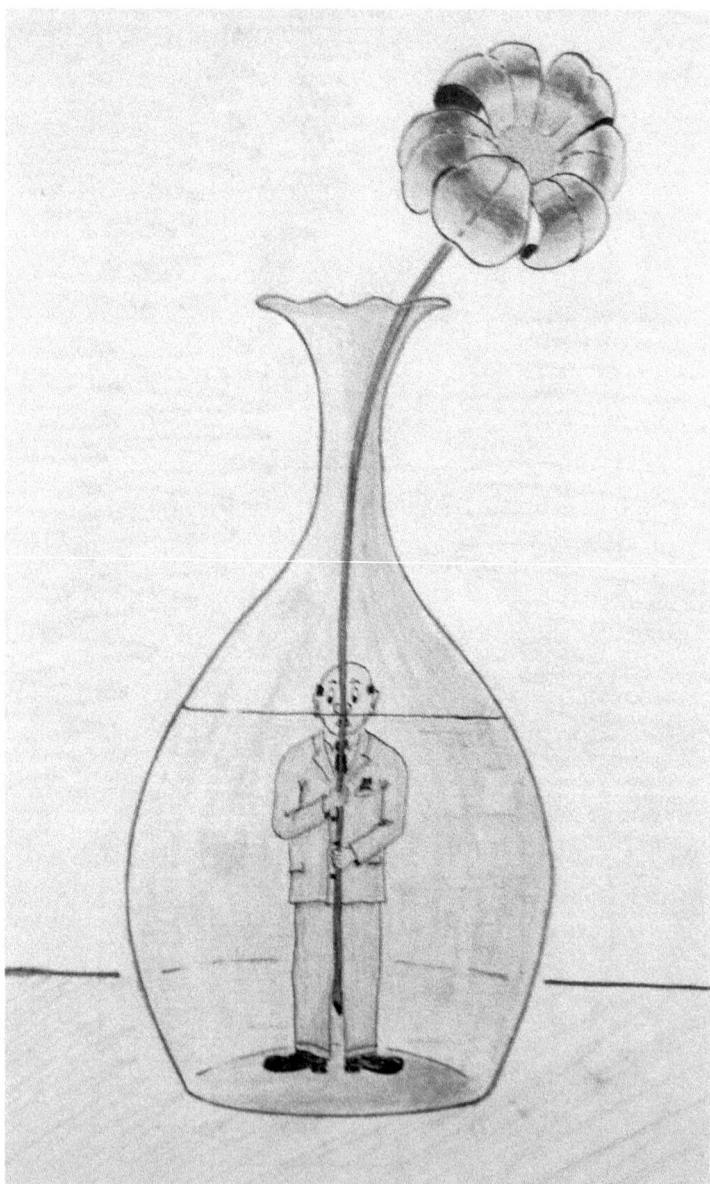

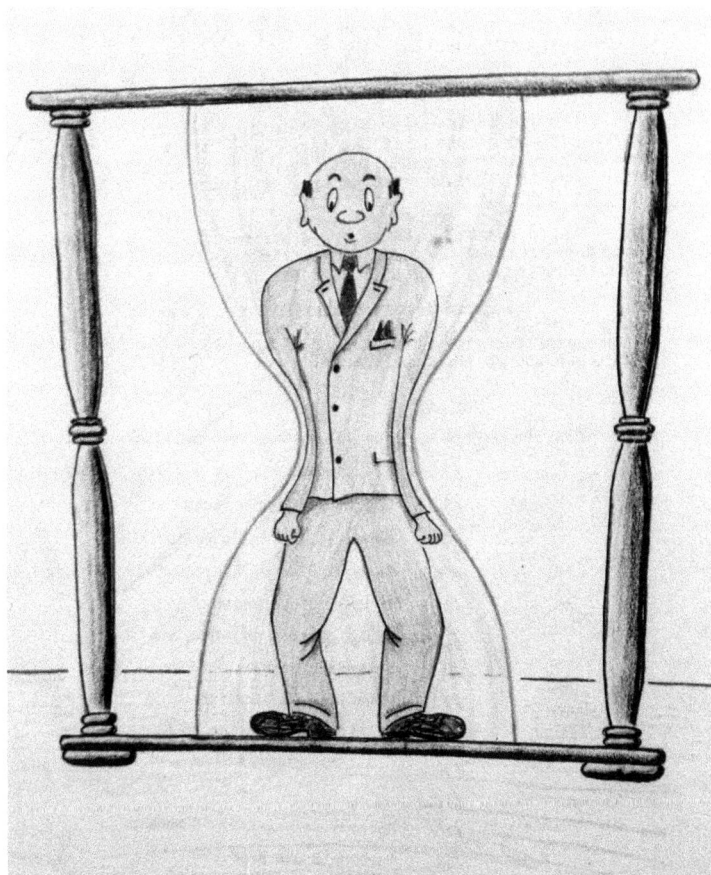

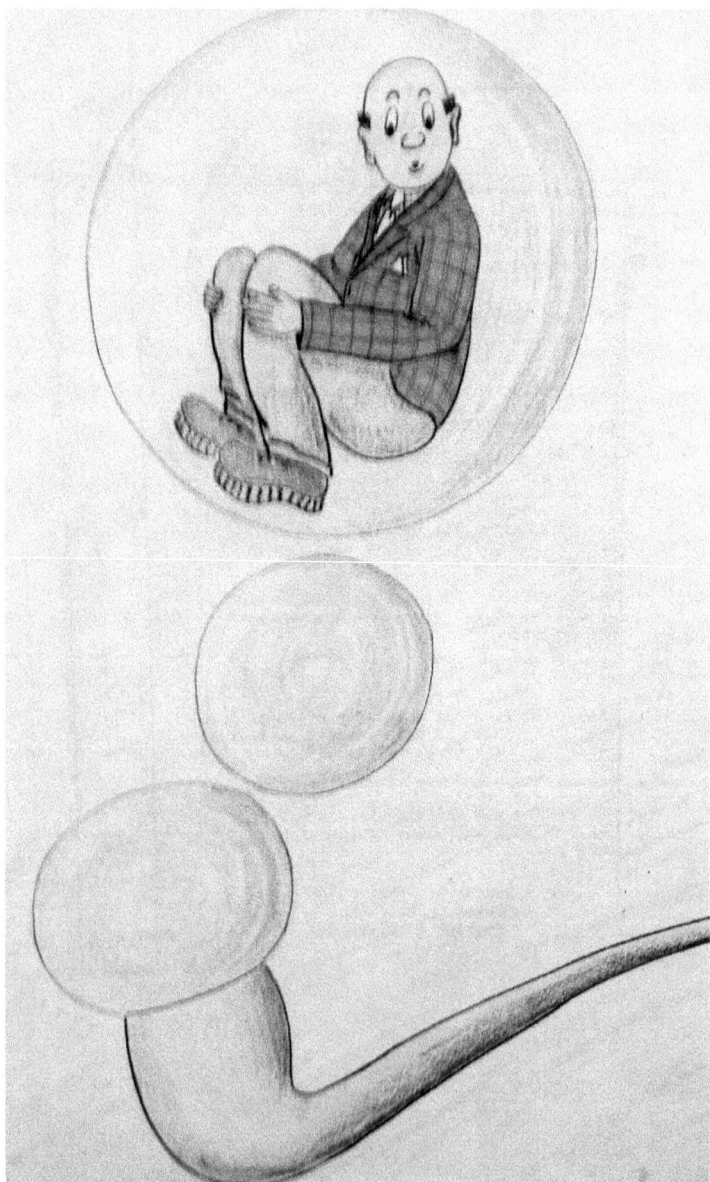

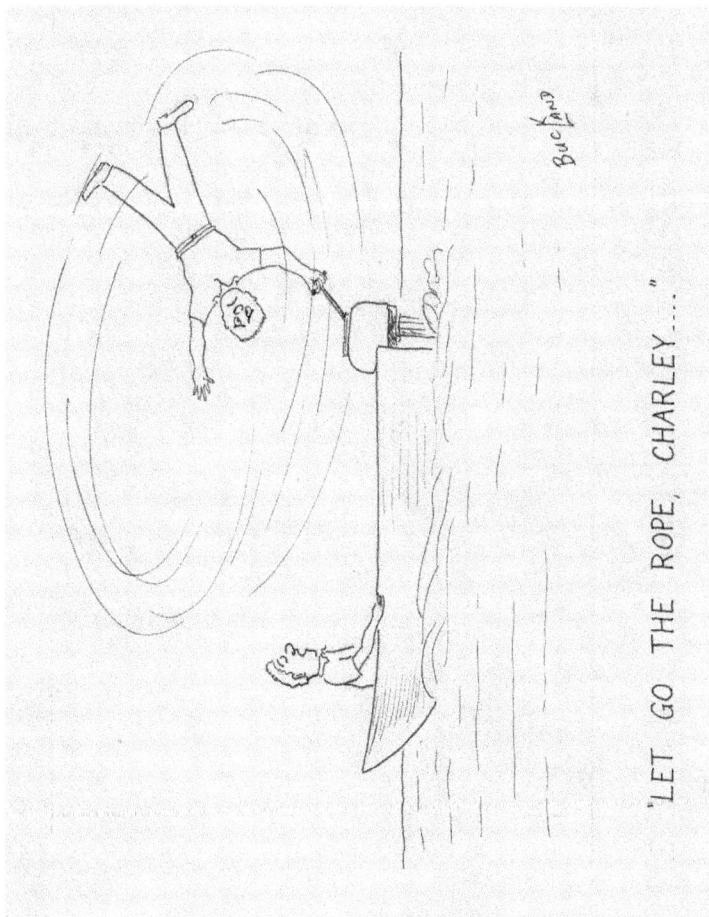

"LET GO THE ROPE, CHARLEY...."

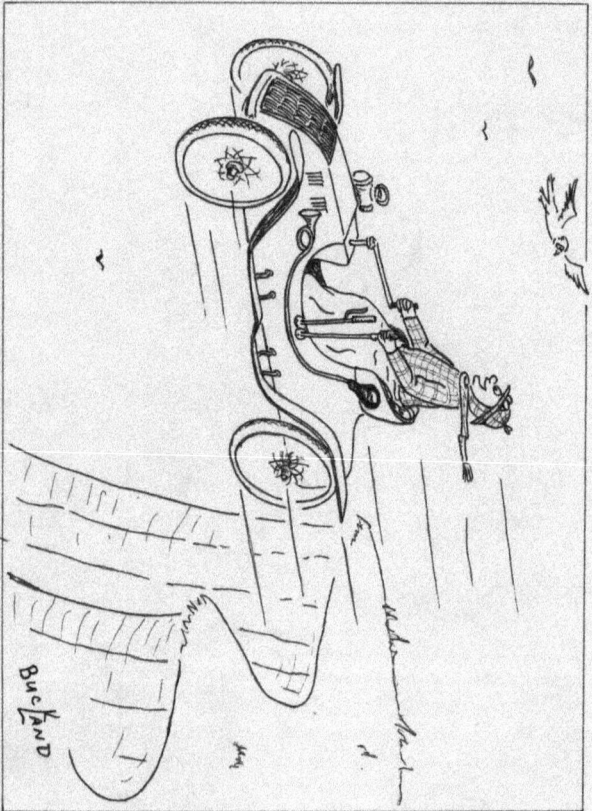

"TO THINK THAT ONE DAY MAN MAY FLY THROUGH THE AIR, AS FREE AS A BIRD!"

"NO SIR,... MEN'S HAIR PIECES ARE OVER AT THE OTHER COUNTER!"

"PREPARE TO FIRE ......"

BuckLAND

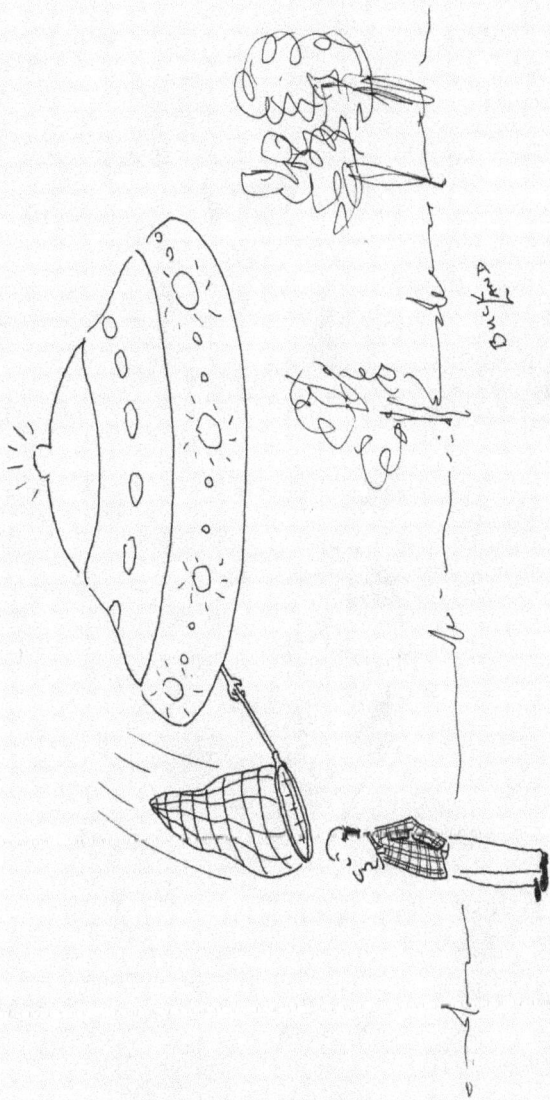

"NO, I DON'T BELIEVE THESE UFO ABDUCTION STORIES!"

"FUNNY HOW BRIGHT IT'S SUDDENLY GOT----!"

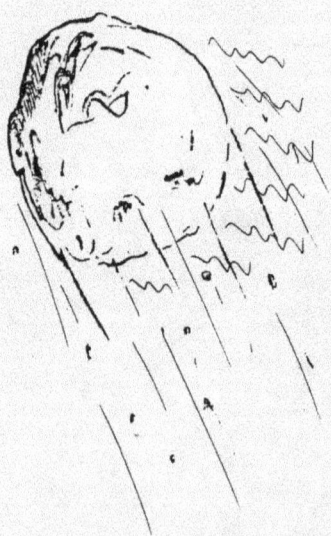

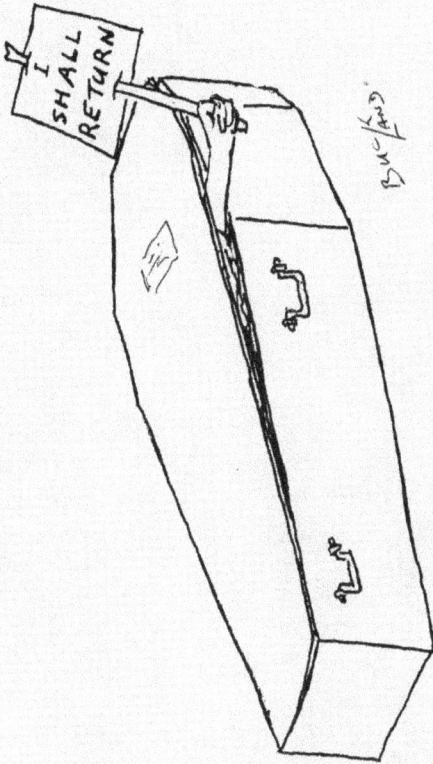

"HERE WE ARE —— NEW 2017 MODEL!"

IMMEDIATE DELIVERY

BUCKLAND

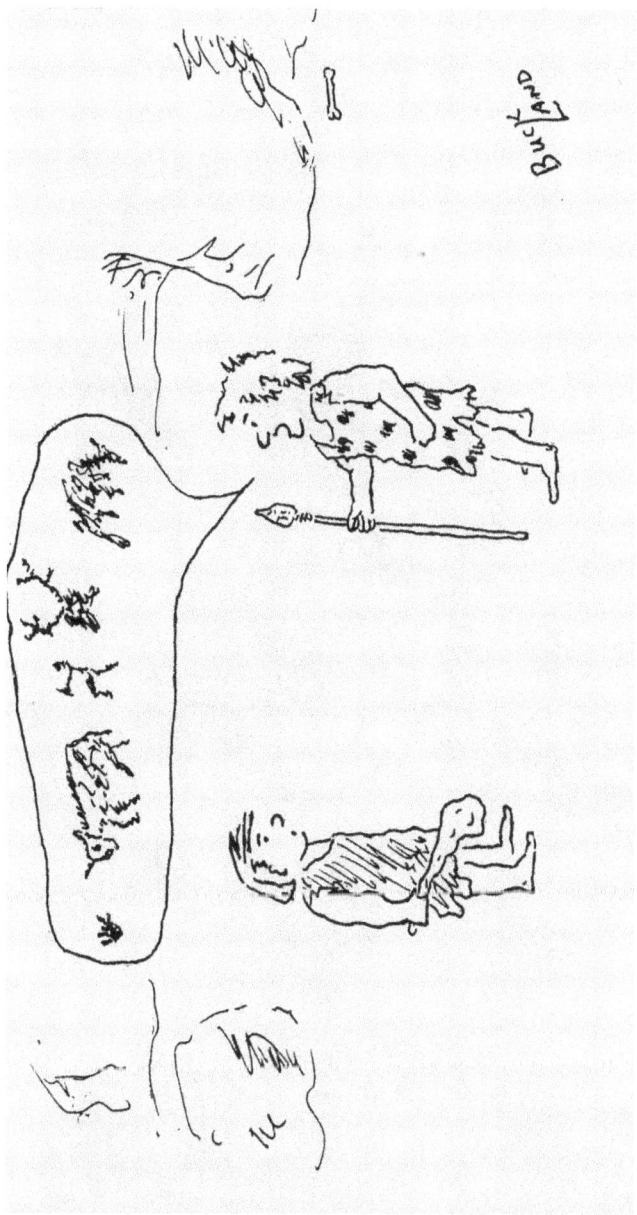

"NO, — PERSONALLY I DO NOT BELIEVE IN THE ABOMINABLE SNOWMAN!"

RAMSES FUNERAL HOME
PARTIES CATERED FOR

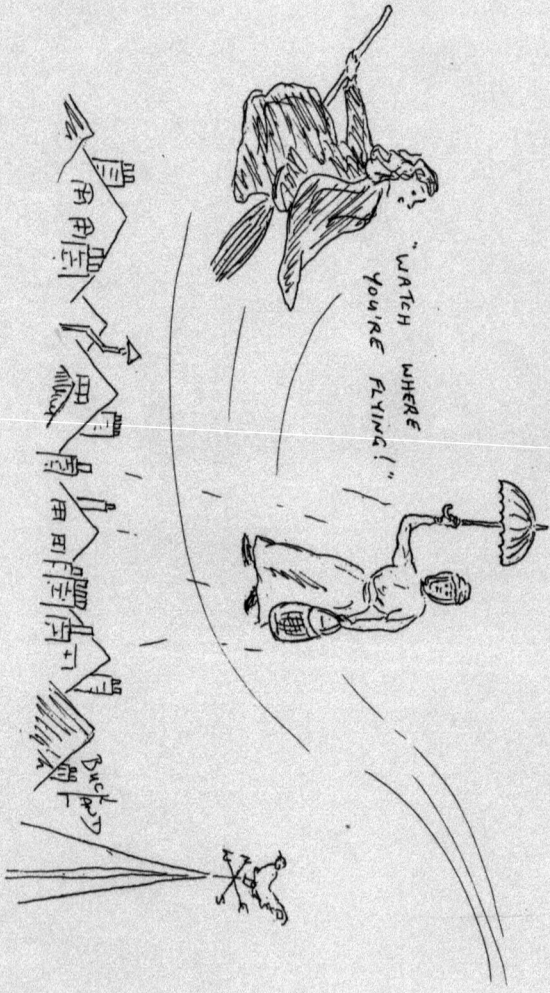

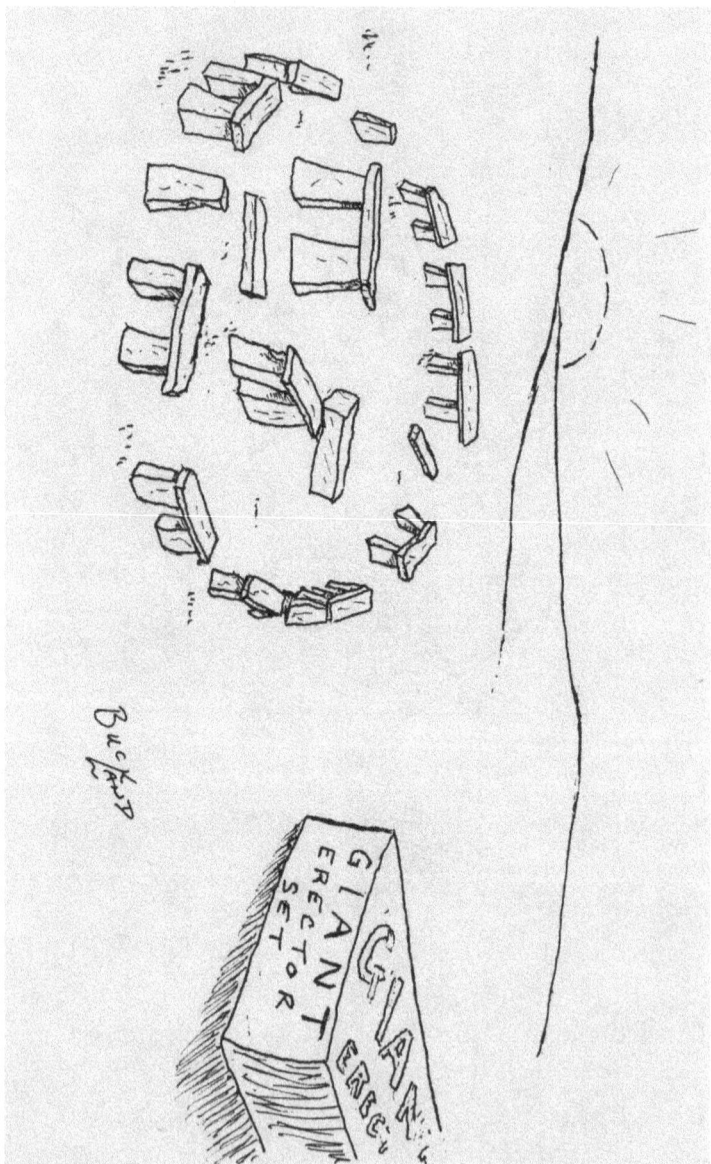

GIANT ERECTOR SET

Buckard

"SEE WHAT I'VE INVENTED!"

"The only way we can get away with wearing this stuff, guys, is to start a band!"

BuckLand

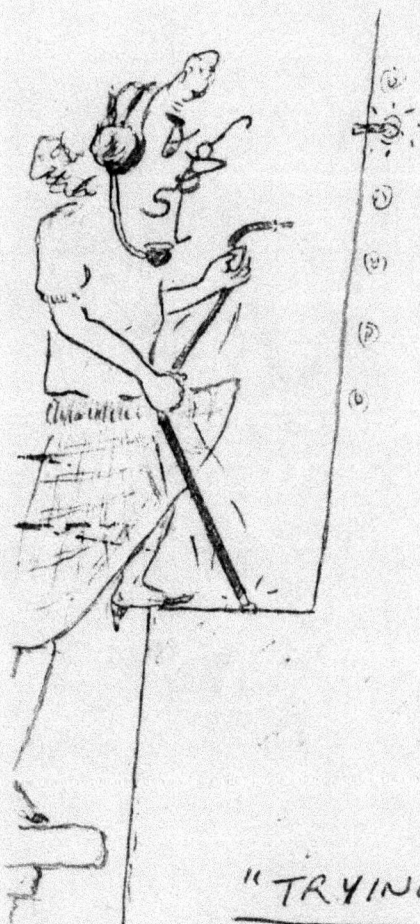

"TRYING TO CONNECT YOU...!"

OLAF
A FIERCE
VIKING —
TERROR
OF THE
SEAS!

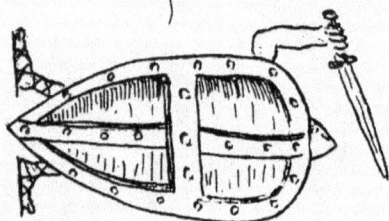

"COME ON OUT AND FIGHT LIKE A MAN!"

"ON THE OTHER HAND IT COULD BE JUST A SHAGGY COW!"

"I CALL IT A L-O-N-G BOAT"

"REMEMBER, SO LONG AS YOU HIT THE TARGET NO ONE CAN GET HURT!"

"RIGHT! — NOW SAY 'CHEESE'!"

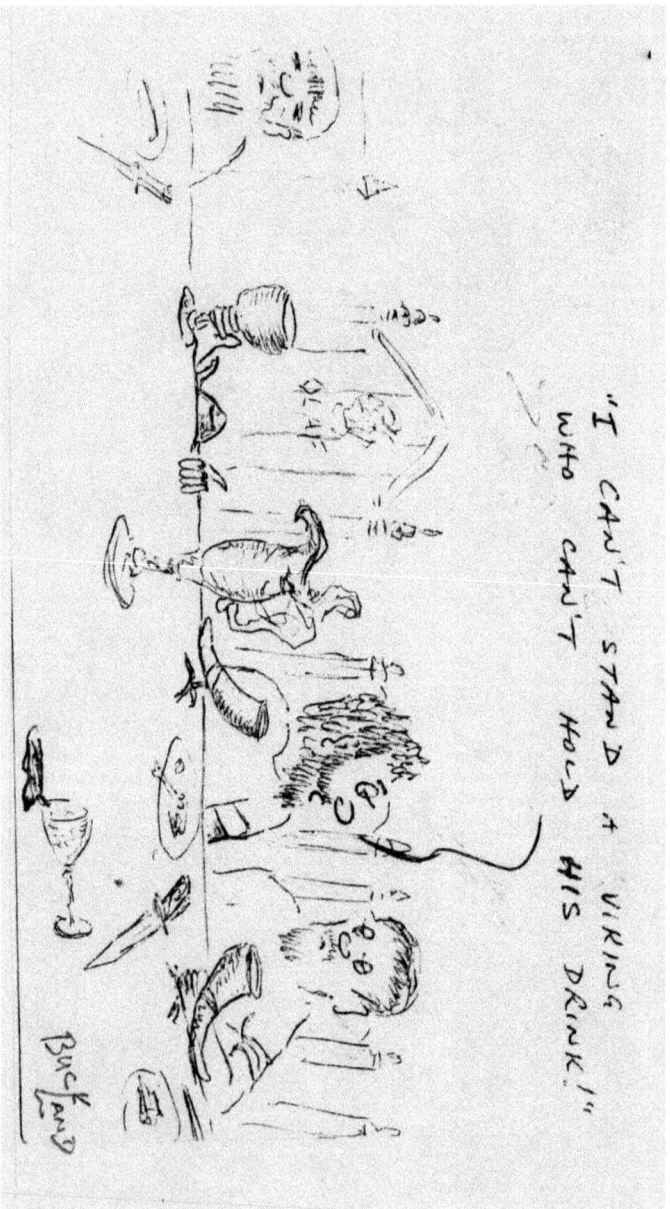

"I CAN'T STAND A VIKING WHO CAN'T HOLD HIS DRINK!"

"AS I ALWAYS SAY, WOMEN AND POLITICS JUST DON'T GO TOGETHER!"

"OLAF JUST CLIMBED UP THE
MAST TO FIX THE SAIL----
NEVER MIND!"

"I DON'T GIVE A DAMN ABOUT
'ARTISTIC FEELING' — WHEN
I ORDER STRIPED SAILS
I WANT STRIPED SAILS!"

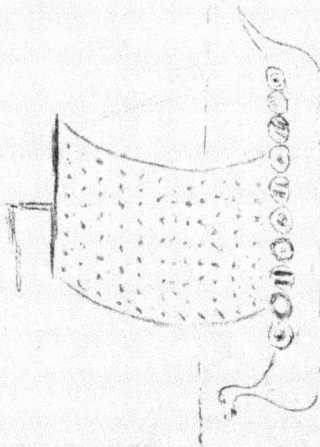

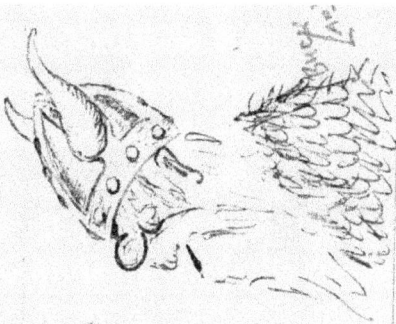

"WHO ARE YOU
CALLING 'DROOPY'?"

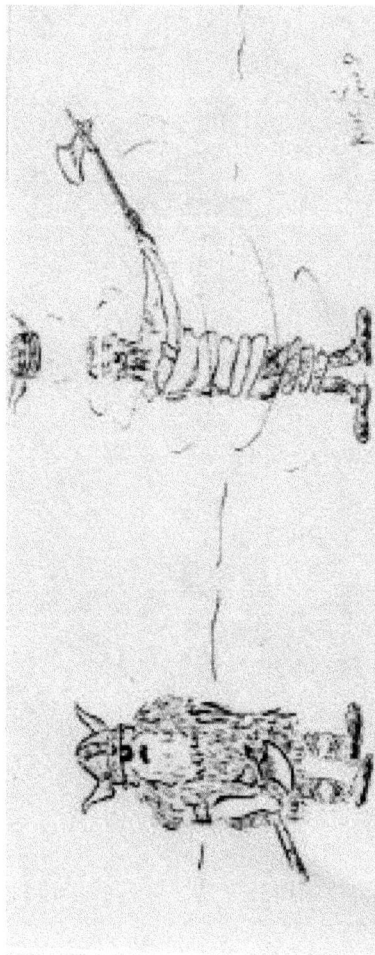

"SURE YOU HAVE A POWERFUL SWING, ERIK, BUT THERE ARE STILL A FEW THINGS YOU NEED TO LEARN...!"

"AND YOU MIGHT WIDEN YOUR DOORWAY A COUPLE OF INCHES, TOO!"

"WOULD YOU BELIEVE, TEXAS LONGHORN?"

"WOULD 'WILLIAM TELL' CARE TO STEP OUTSIDE A MOMENT?"

"LIKE I ALWAYS SAY,
YOU CAN'T KEEP A GOOD
VIKING AWAY FROM THE SEA!"

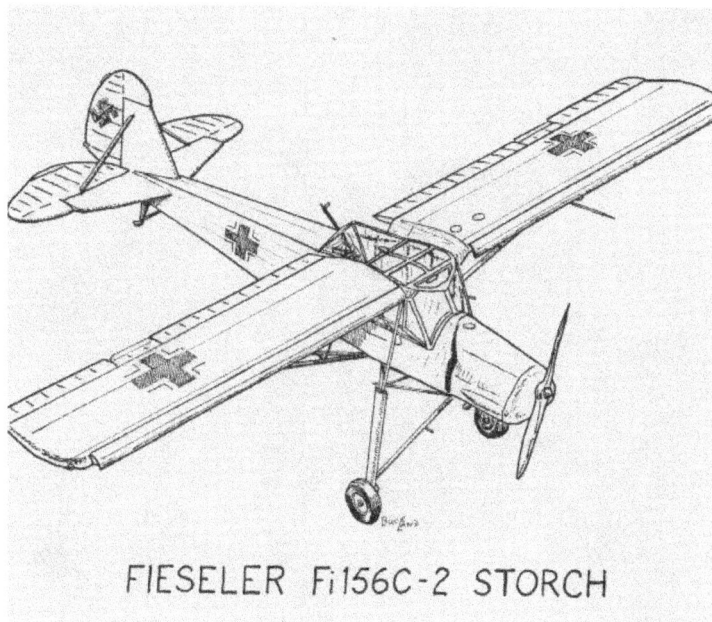

FIESELER Fi156C-2 STORCH

"ACTUALLY YOU SHOULD LET GO AS SOON AS THE ENGINE FIRES!"

"I BET YOU DIDN'T KNOW I WAS GOING TO DO A LOOP, DID YOU, HARRY?"

"IT HAS BEEN REQUESTED THAT WE REMOVE OUR HELMETS BEFORE BOARDING THE ZEPPERLIN!"

BUCKLAND

'NOW TRY A LOOP,' HE SAID —
'BY THE WAY' HE SAID, 'YOU
HAVE STRAPPED YOURSELF IN,
HAVEN'T YOU?' HE SAID.....!

BUCKLAND

"I must count to ten before pulling the ripcord ... I must count to ten before pulling the ripcord ... I must count to ten before ....."

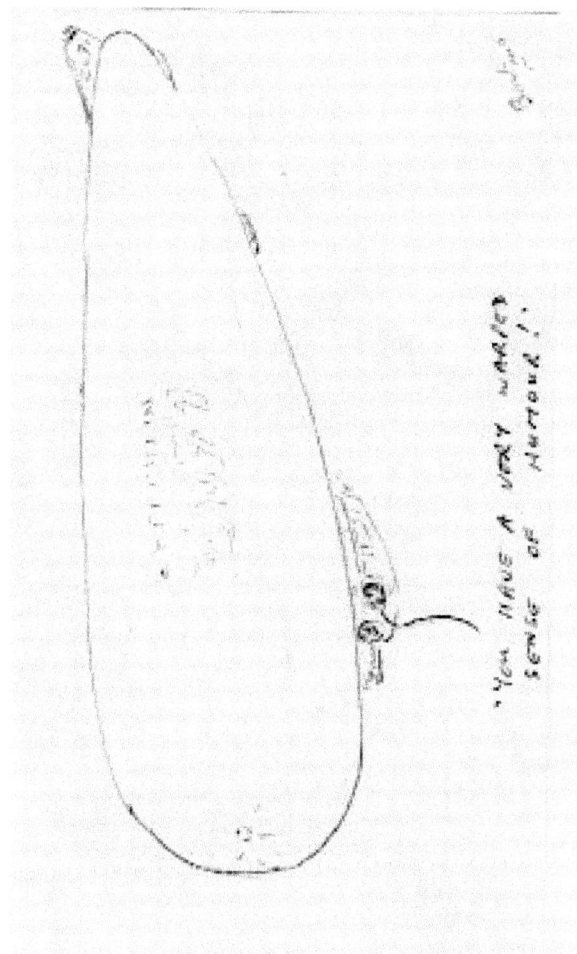

"YOU HAVE A VERY WARPED SENSE OF HUMOUR !"

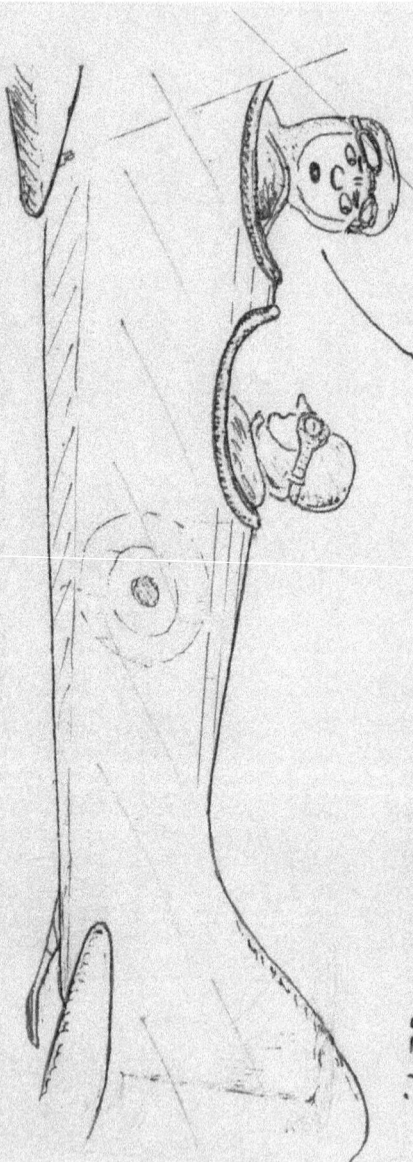

"I SAID I'LL BE DAMN GLAD WHEN THEY INVENT THE JET!"

Buckland

"DAMN WOMEN DRIVERS!"

"AW, COME ON UP HIGHER DAD — WHERE'S YOUR SPIRIT OF ADVENTURE?"

BUCKLAND

"ON THE OTHER HAND, IT COULD BE JUST A NEW TYPE RADIO ANTENNA?!"

BUCKLAND

"AND WHAT DOES THIS BUTTON DO?"

BUCKARD

"PULL WHAT RIPCORD?...
ON WHAT PARACHUTE?"

"WHEN WE FLY THROUGH A HANGAR, THON FROM, WE MAKE SURE BOTH ENDS ARE OPEN!"

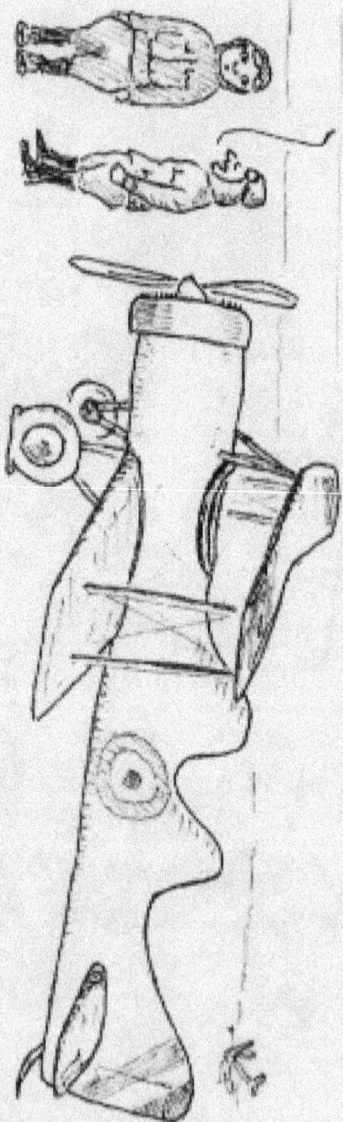

"I CALL IT THE SOPWITH CAMEL"

"I BET YOU DIDN'T KNOW I WAS GOING TO DO A LOOP, DID YOU, HARRY?"

"HAVE YOU EVER THOUGHT OF TRYING TO LOSE SOME WEIGHT?!"

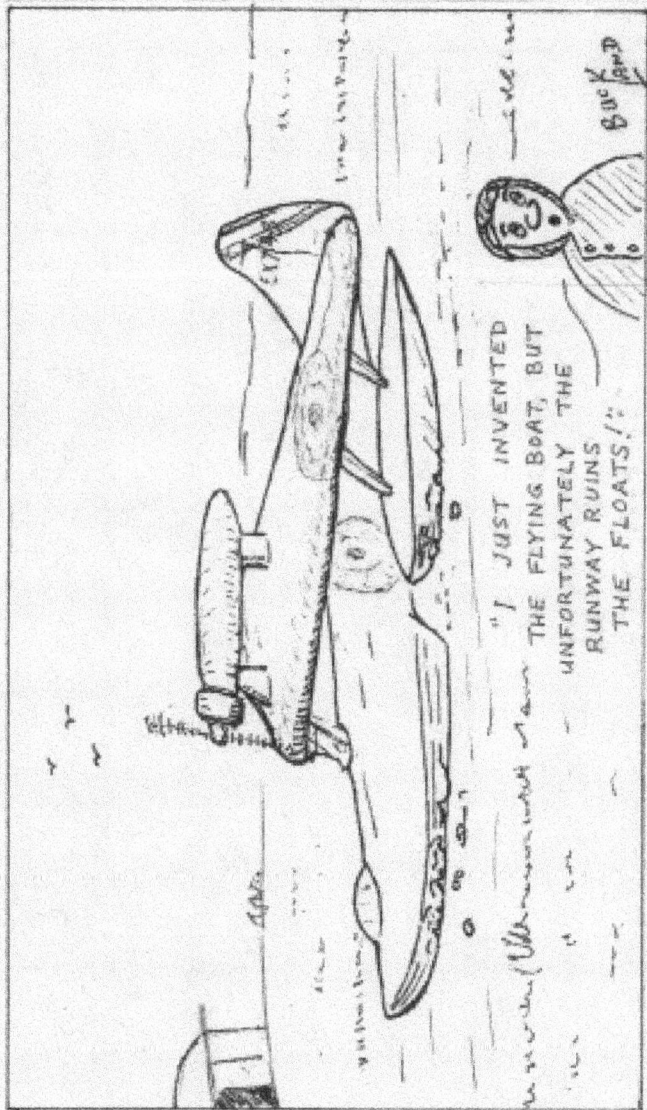

"I JUST INVENTED THE FLYING BOAT, BUT UNFORTUNATELY THE RUNWAY RUINS THE FLOATS!"

BucKland

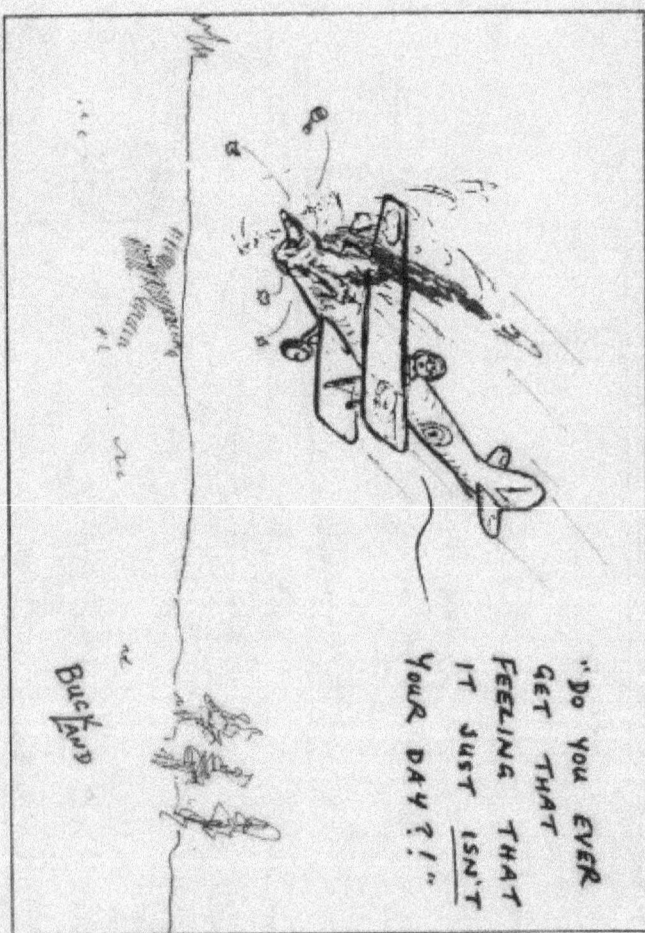

"DO YOU EVER GET THAT FEELING THAT IT JUST ISN'T YOUR DAY?!"

"DON'T FORGET TO LET GO OF THE ROPE, GEORGE!"

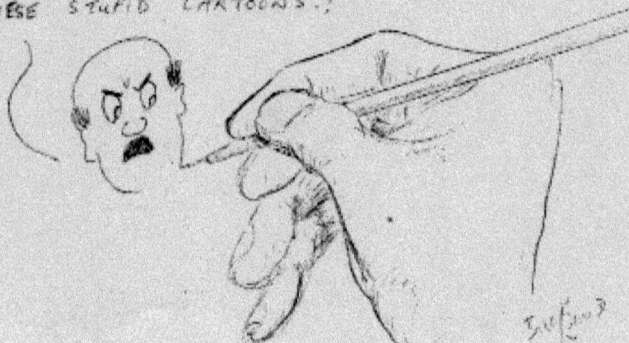

QUEEN VICTORIA PRESS

Fiction by Raymond Buckland
A MISTAKE THROUGH THE HEART – Book Three of the
Bram Stoker Mysteries
CHURCHILL'S SECRET SPY – WWII espionage
THE PENNY COURT ENQUIRERS – Victorian mystery series
  1: One Clue at a Time
  2: The Noble Savage
  3: Deadly Spirit
PARANORMAL POETRY – A chapbook of poetry strange
and unusual
OUT OF THIS WORLD – A collection of science-fiction short
stories
LAFF WITH OLAF & Others – a book of cartoons
In Preparation:
  THE WIITIKO INHERITANCE
  THE SECRET LIFE OF MISS EMMELINE CROMWELL
Non-fiction by Raymond Buckland
WITCHCRAFT REVEALED – An examination of Witchcraft
and Wicca
OUIJA CONNECTION TO SPIRIT – The talking board and
how to contact the Spirit World
PARANORMAL PRIMER – A "how-to" on many popular
metaphysical practices
HERE IS THE OCCULT – An introduction to the wide world
of the Paranormal
In Preparation:
THE BOOK OF ALCHEMY
THE CARDS OF ALCHEMY
PSYCHIC WORLD SECRETS
ANATOMY OF THE PARANORMAL

www.queenvictoriapress.com

www.ingramcontent.com/pod-product-compliance
Lightning Source LLC
Chambersburg PA
CBHW070539030426
42337CB00016B/2276